A BOOK OF DAYS

A BOOK OF DAYS

———

patti smith

RANDOM HOUSE
New York

Published in the United States by Random House,
an imprint and division of Penguin Random House LLC, New York.

RANDOM HOUSE and the HOUSE colophon are registered
trademarks of Penguin Random House LLC.

Photograph credits appear on page 383.

Hardback ISBN 978-0-593-44854-0
Ebook ISBN 978-0-593-44855-7

Printed in Italy on acid-free paper

randomhousebooks.com

2 4 6 8 9 7 5 3 1

First Edition

Book design by Debbie Glasserman

A hundred thousand birds salute the day.

CHRISTINA GEORGINA ROSSETTI

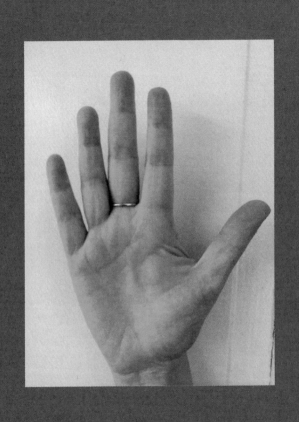

HELLO EVERYBODY

On March 20, 2018, the Spring Equinox, I posted my first Instagram entry. My daughter, Jesse, had suggested that I open an Instagram account to distinguish mine from fraudulent ones soliciting in my name. Jesse also felt the platform would suit me, as I write and take pictures every day. She and I created the site together. I wondered how I might signal to the people that it was truly me reaching out to them. I decided upon a straightforward approach: thisispattismith.

I used my own hand as the image for my first venture into the virtual world. The hand is one of the oldest of icons, a direct correspondence between imagination and execution. Healing energy is channeled through our hands. We extend a hand in greeting and service; we raise a hand as a pledge. Ocher handprints, thousands of years old, found stenciled in the Chauvet–Pont d'Arc Cave in southeastern France, were formed by spitting red pigment over a hand pressed against the stone wall to merge with an element of strength or perhaps to signal a prehistoric declaration of self.

Instagram has served as a way to share old and new discoveries, celebrate birthdays, remember the departed, and salute our youth. I write my captions in a notebook or directly on the phone. I would have liked to have had a Polaroid-based site, but as the film has been discontinued, my camera is now a retired witness of former travels. The images in this book are drawn from existing Polaroids, my archive, and the cellphone. A process unique to the twenty-first century.

Although I miss my camera and the specific atmosphere of the Polaroid image, I appreciate the flexibility of the cellphone. My first inkling of a cellphone's possible artistic usefulness was through Annie Leibovitz. In 2004 she took an interior shot with her cell, and then printed it out as a small, low-resolution image. She said offhandedly that she thought it would one day be possible to take worthy pictures with a phone. I didn't consider having a cellphone back then, but we evolve with the times. Mine, acquired in 2010, has enabled me to unite with the exploding collage of our culture.

A Book of Days is a glimpse of how I navigate this culture in my own way. It was inspired by my Instagram but is uniquely its own. Much of it I created during the pandemic, in my room alone, projecting into the future and reflecting the past, family, and a consistent personal aesthetic.

Entries and images are keys to unlocking one's own thoughts. Each is surrounded with the reverberation of other possibilities. Birthdays acknowledged are prompts for others, including your own. A Paris café is all cafés, just as a gravesite may echo others mourned and remembered. Having experienced much loss, I've found solace in frequenting the cemeteries of people I love, and I have visited many, offering my prayers, respect, and gratitude. I am at home with history and tracing the steps of those whose work has inspired me; many entries are that of remembrance.

I have been encouraged in watching my site grow, from the first follower, my daughter, to over one million. This book, a year and a day (for those born on leap day), is offered in gratitude, as a place to be heartened, even in the basest of times. Each day is precious, for we are yet breathing, moved by the way light falls on a high branch, or a morning worktable, or the sculpted headstone of a beloved poet.

Social media, in its twisting of democracy, sometimes courts cruelty, reactionary commentary, misinformation, and nationalism, but it can also serve us. It's in our hands. The hand that composes a message, smooths a child's hair, pulls back the arrow and lets it fly. Here are my arrows aiming for the common heart of things. Each attached with a few words, scrappy oracles.

Three hundred and sixty-six ways of saying hello.

JANUARY

01 JANUARY

A new year is unfolding, the unknown before us,
brimming with possibilities.

02 JANUARY

After a day of rest, we take a moment to ask ourselves what we
hope to accomplish. Small vows, urgent promises to be useful,
to be better, to shed what is not needed.

03 JANUARY

Greta Thunberg pledged her childhood to Activism.
Nature knows and smiles upon her on her birthday.

04 JANUARY

This humble headstone marks the resting place of writer
Albert Camus, a proud and singular man.

05 JANUARY

My armor.

06 JANUARY

Divinely commissioned to liberate France from England's
clutches, Joan of Arc left her country home in search of horse,
sword, and a suit of armor. At nineteen, guided by saints, she
accomplished her mission, then was betrayed and burned at
the stake. On her birthday, we are reminded of the principled
and ardent fervor of youth.

07 JANUARY

As the bells of Ghent toll, a long stroll beyond the bridge
of St. Michael. Then spending a while in the church of
St. Nicholas, as the pipe organ bellows songs of obscure
prophets with golden saws and saints with swords and the
keys to heaven.

08 JANUARY

As a young girl, I admired the skater's attire, adopting the
look as my own. Black coat, black tights, white collar. The
plate belonged to my mother, who preferred me in bright
colors, but the skater prevailed. He dwells beside my copy
of *Ariel*, another significant influence, given to me by
Robert Mapplethorpe in 1968.

09 JANUARY

She has given the lion's share of her eighty years toward the elevation of the human condition. She never let us down, by action or example. Her fearless voice a bell tolling for equality, opposing war, empowering the downtrodden. Happy birthday, Joan Baez, our dark butterfly.

10 JANUARY

This was a favorite book from my childhood: *Around the World in 1,000 Pictures*. In 1954, I began keeping a list of all the places I wished to go. Providence has been kind, and with camera in hand, I've been to many of them. I retrace my steps through yellowed pages, much thumbed by a dreamy twelve-year-old girl.

11 JANUARY

My first view of a palm was in the book of 1,000 pictures.
In my travels I have seen many, such as this curved palm
in San Juan.

12 JANUARY

A Polaroid of Haruki Murakami in Tokyo. He has said that there is no such thing as perfect writing, just as there is no such thing as perfect despair. Exquisitely imperfect Murakami! On his birthday, I imagine him waking in a great silver capsule, descending the stairs, and looking up at a brilliant yellow sky.

13 JANUARY

This is one of the waterwheels built by the great Akira
Kurosawa for his final film, *Dreams*. He did not dismantle
them, as the people had grown to love them. They turn in the
water in the Japanese Alps, where wasabi grows. I went there
to see for myself the wheels that manifested from Kurosawa's
dreams. An arduous search for simplicity that was well rewarded.

14 JANUARY

Ocean Grove, Winter.

15 JANUARY

The arc of the moral universe is long, but it bends toward justice.

—MARTIN LUTHER KING JR.,

JANUARY 15, 1929–APRIL 4, 1968

16 JANUARY

The desk of the great writer Jorge Luis Borges lives in the National Library in Buenos Aires. It was designed to encompass him, perhaps to assist in reining in his infinitely expansive universe.

17 JANUARY

In a preserved corner of the Café Tortoni, surrounded by
Belle Epoch décor, a tableau immortalizes the great Borges,
joined by tango singer Carlos Gardel and the poet Alfonsina
Storni. A wax-museum diorama, coffee in perpetuity.

18 JANUARY

London. Florence. Hiroshima.

19 JANUARY

This is my Polaroid Land 250 with a Zeiss range finder. My
idiosyncratic working companion for two decades of travel.
With film discontinued it is now obsolete, yet holds a place of
prominence among my work tools. Nothing really matches the
atmosphere of the old Polaroid film. Except perhaps a poem,
a musical phrase, or a forest hung with mist.

20 JANUARY

The hand, the stroke of the pen, words funneling.

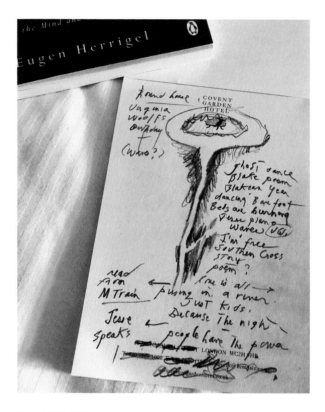

21 JANUARY

A setlist is the spine of a performance, a guide for each night.
It is part of our process; my bass player Tony Shanahan and I
feel a sense of the night, its atmosphere and the energy of the
people, and prepare the list, the concert's inner narrative.

22 JANUARY

Fondation Cartier pour l'art contemporain, Paris. My son
Jackson, stoic and assured, playing in his favorite shirt.

23 JANUARY

This is Ravi Coltrane and Steve Jordan, setting up with their
fellow musicians to soar in "Expression," a composition by
Ravi's father, the great master John Coltrane. Music sings in
the blood of our sons.

24 JANUARY

Monk's House, Rodmell. In the garden where her ashes are
buried, a bust of Virginia Woolf, cloaked in ivy, silently reigns.

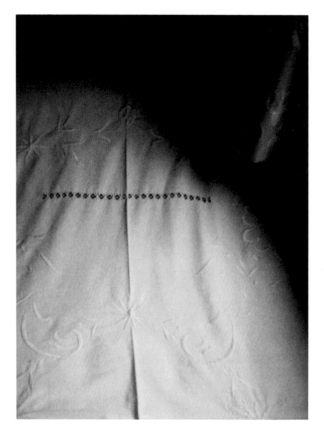

25 JANUARY

Virginia Woolf, born January 25, 1882.
This is her dreaming bed.

26 JANUARY

On the anniversary of the poet and wanderer Gérard de
Nerval's death, I offer the opening line of his *Aurélia*—
Our dreams are a second life. A writer's mantra.

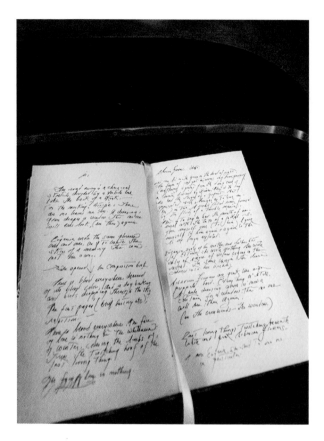

27 JANUARY

Reading Nerval has always inspired me to write. This is the
greatest gift that an artist bequeaths to future artists, igniting
the desire to produce their own work.

28 JANUARY

Desk talismans: a postcard image of Mark Rothko.
A St. Francis tau from a monk in Assisi. Sam Shepard's
pocketknife. A gold-flecked Murano bowl from Dimitri.
Keep on going, no matter what, my talismans seem to whisper.

29 JANUARY

Thinking of nothing. I remember my mother sitting like this.
And I would ask, What is it, Mommy? And she would say,
Oh nothing. And now I know what nothing is.

30 JANUARY

Facing the chaos of mounting books, manuscripts, and just plain mess that always accrues when I'm deeply concentrating on something else. Today, I sorted, purged, and cleaned up. Not much fun but I managed to make a game of it, pretending my organizational skills were being observed by aliens.

31 JANUARY

Now, all done, and escaping abduction, I am ready to begin
new work, primed to make a new mess.

FEBRUARY

01 FEBRUARY

Jesse with roses in the snow.

02 FEBRUARY

My desk in winter light.

03 FEBRUARY

Introducing Cairo, my Abyssinian. A sweet little thing the color of the pyramids, with a loyal and peaceful disposition.

04 FEBRUARY

Gem Spa, a corner newsstand that served us twenty-four
hours a day for decades. The spot for underground newspapers,
foreign cigarettes, and candy bars. Robert Mapplethorpe
bought me my first chocolate egg cream there in August 1967.
Everyone passed through its open door, now closed, the beats
and hippies and us, just kids.

05 FEBRUARY

This is with William Burroughs at his Bunker on the
Bowery, taken by Allen Ginsberg on September 20, 1975.
I miss walking by his side, always pleased and proud to do so.
Happy birthday, dear William, may your golden sails reach
the port of saints.

06 FEBRUARY

Stacking end tables, dreaming of Constantin Brancusi's
Endless Column.

07 FEBRUARY

Beverly Pepper was an American sculptor who made her home in Todi, Umbria. Her work stands monumental, her spirit unfettered. With the future uncertain, she stated that she worked in the present as projected from the past, her own brand of futurism.

08 FEBRUARY

Independence Hall, Philadelphia. The Declaration of
Independence and the Articles of Confederation were ratified
in the City of Brotherly Love, whose cobbled streets I tread
upon as a young girl. The same streets that Thomas Paine
walked while contemplating the rights of his fellow citizens.

09 FEBRUARY

Thomas Paine, writer, philosopher, and revolutionary, penned "The world is my country, all mankind are my brethren, and to do good is my religion." He spoke out against slavery and the growing tyranny of religion. Shunned for being too outspoken, he died alone and penniless. On his birthday, we revisit this radiant thinker, standard-bearer for common sense.

10 FEBRUARY

The surreal reality of the relentlessly breathtaking
Icelandic terrain.

11 FEBRUARY

A white Iceland pony appeared in the distance, as if
the unicorn had broken through the metallic threads of
the cloister's storied tapestry.

12 FEBRUARY

Still life with *Finnegans Wake*, a bible of the incomprehensible, by the great Irish writer James Joyce. I obtained it some years ago in a London bookshop with money I earned performing poetry. Joyce labored on his masterwork for seventeen years, so one need not hurry to navigate it.

13 FEBRUARY

The key is equally incomprehensible.

Their eyes are fires
just half put out
Their hearts sway
open like their doors.

♥

14 FEBRUARY

Robert was my Valentine. February 14, 1968.

15 FEBRUARY

Robert gave me this Persian necklace, wrapped in black tissue.

16 FEBRUARY

Germantown, Pennsylvania, 1952. Sisters. True love.

17 FEBRUARY

Washington Square, New York City. This amiable fellow
produced a nostalgic desire for mismatched mittens and
welcoming mugs of steaming cocoa.

18 FEBRUARY

As a young girl she lived through bombings and starvation in war-torn Japan. Seeing the ravages of war, the terrible destruction and desperation, made a deep, lasting impression, impacting her unique voice as an artist and activist. On Yoko Ono's birthday, may all give peace a chance.

19 FEBRUARY

This is the Peace Pagoda in Japantown, San Francisco. The
strange weather gave everything the inner glow and aura of
another time, the tower emerging from the mist like an old
postcard faded in the sun.

20 FEBRUARY

In his fleeting life all aspects of his work embodied the sacred
and damned duality of being a rock and roll star.
Kurt Cobain, February 20, 1967–April 5, 1994.

21 FEBRUARY

Rabbit news courtesy of Lewis Carroll and Grace Slick.
Remember the dodo. Feed your head.

22 FEBRUARY

This is the hat of the poet Lawrence Ferlinghetti.
No other shall wear it.

23 FEBRUARY

Rockaway Beach. Restless gulls, restless hearts.

24 FEBRUARY

My sister's sewing basket, spools of a humble seamstress.

25 FEBRUARY

Lincoln death mask. We honor his elegant simplicity.

26 FEBRUARY

This was my father's cup. On occasion he would call us into
the kitchen, pour some coffee, then read aloud "Abou Ben
Adhem," by Leigh Hunt. It contained his personal philosophy
that seems fixed within his empty cup.

27 FEBRUARY

Happy birthday to Ralph Nader, whom my father admired for his lifelong service to the people. He felt that Ralph lived up to the words in his favorite poem. "Write me as one that loves his fellow men."

28 FEBRUARY

With Lenny Kaye by the sea, Byron Bay, Australia.
Fifty years of work and friendship.

29 FEBRUARY

Fred Sonic Smith and I made a wish on this date as the full
moon rose over Michigan; the following day we leapt into our
new life. Thinking of that night, I sometimes toss a coin in my
old Spanish well, sending future leap year wishes to all.

MARCH

01 MARCH

With Fred before the Mariners' Church of Detroit, where we
were wed on March 1, 1980. When alchemy was real.

02 MARCH

This table was used in the famed World Chess Championship
between Bobby Fischer and Boris Spassky in Reykjavik,
Iceland, in 1972. Though the table is modest in appearance,
every move made on its board reverberated around the world,
as the brilliant upstart Fischer royally defeated Spassky, the
reigning champion from the Soviet Union.

03 MARCH

This is the grave of Bobby Fischer. As he craved solitude,
he chose to be buried next to a small white clapboard church
near the village of Selfoss, a stone's throw from where
Iceland ponies graze.

04 MARCH

These photographs of Antonin Artaud by Georges Pastier
were kept in a cigar box near Artaud's bed in the asylum in
Ivry-sur-Seine where he died. I imagine the poet alone in his
room gazing at them, the double of himself.

05 MARCH

Happily working with the gentle and indefatigable
Werner Herzog on English and German interpretations
of Artaud's *Peyote Dance* for Soundwalk Collective at the
historic Electric Lady Studios.

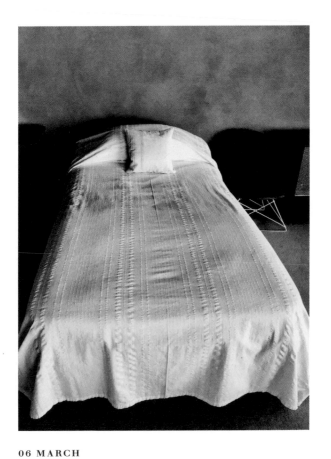

06 MARCH

Georgia O'Keeffe's bed.

07 MARCH

Everything in the adobe dwelling and studio in Abiquiú
breathes of Georgia O'Keeffe. The surface of the walls, the
ladder, the surrounding landscape, and the dry bones beyond.

08 MARCH

On International Women's Day we remember the graceful
Iranian mathematician Maryam Mirzakhani, the only woman
to win the Fields Medal, mathematics' highest honor. She
was the maestro of curved spaces, and one can barely conceive
of the celestial landscape of her elastic mind. Mirzakhani died
of cancer at the age of forty, counted in the stars as the queen
of geometric imagination.

09 MARCH

Jesse on the march.

10 MARCH

All I needed in Paris.

11 MARCH

Rockaway Beach. My trusty CD player is all I need to listen to
my favorite music. In another corner, awaiting rotation, are
Ornette Coleman, Philip Glass, Marvin Gaye, and REM.

12 MARCH

At the Waldorf Astoria hotel with Michael Stipe. We were
about to be inducted into the Rock & Roll Hall of Fame, and
entered the ballroom together, each comprehending the other.

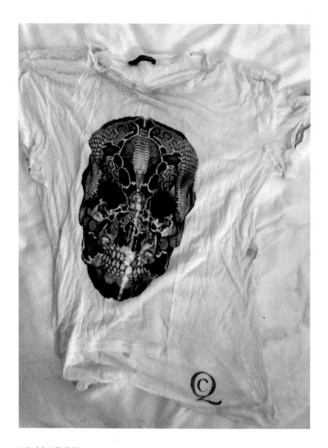

13 MARCH

The Alexander McQueen T-shirt given to me by Michael upon
the designer's death. I have worn it so many times performing,
thinking of McQueen, the Mozart of cloth.

14 MARCH

On the birthday of photographer Diane Arbus, I am spending
time with *Revelations,* a magnificent presentation of her work
and process. Gazing at her face, I picture her in 1970, entering
the lobby of the Chelsea Hotel with a manifest sense of
purpose and ever-present camera, her third eye.

15 MARCH

My bed in Rockaway.

16 MARCH

Wo Hop in Chinatown, frequented by musicians for over
eighty years. In the early seventies, after a third set at CBGB,
we'd all head to 17 Mott Street, where the wooden tables held
the scent of oolong tea, and a big bowl of duck congee cost
under a dollar. It still remains, below the stairs, visited by
hungry ghosts.

17 MARCH

My bass player Tony Shanahan, the son of Irish immigrants. His father was a revered baker; Tony has the flour and soil of Ireland dusting his musician hands.

18 MARCH

My cup, a gift from Jesse.

19 MARCH

This is my mother, Beverly Williams Smith, who gave me life and guided my first steps.

20 MARCH

The Vernal Equinox ushers in World Storytelling Day.
This is Sophie Gengembre Anderson's portrait of
Scheherazade, literature's most beguiling weaver of tales,
whose stories famously stayed the hand of the sultan, who
fell in love and spared her life. Her legacy is the classic
One Thousand and One Nights.

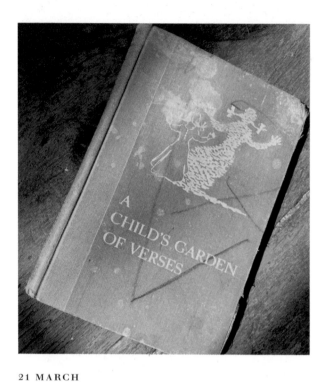

21 MARCH

World Poetry Day. The convalescing child's bible.

22 MARCH

Jay Dee Daugherty, meditative master of cymbals, my
extraordinary drummer since 1975.

23 MARCH

West Virginia. A light snow fell as I listened to the Seventh
Symphony, carried away from all cares.

24 MARCH

The Empire State Building, our queen, was once the world's tallest building. Though now surpassed in height, none has eclipsed her stoic beauty.

25 MARCH

Poet Frank O'Hara—on a lunch break—cigarettes
and telephone.

26 MARCH

This is my other camera, the equalizer.

27 MARCH

Freedom Tower. The geometry of architecture obscured
by cloud.

28 MARCH

Cairo is mesmerized by the history of the medicinal properties of the lemon.

29 MARCH

Taking some time out from spring-cleaning to consult
my childhood mentor, Little Lulu, champion of mischief
and imagination.

30 MARCH

Tokyo. A close encounter with Ultraman.

31 MARCH

Jesse and I making self-pictures.

APRIL

01 APRIL

Today is the birthday of Nikolai Gogol, the great Russian-Ukrainian writer, who once wrote, "A word aptly uttered or written cannot be cut away with an axe."

02 APRIL

Black coat with handkerchief.

03 APRIL

Black coat without its peak.

04 APRIL

The poet Arseny Tarkovsky and his son, Andrei. One can only imagine the interior world of the child who would one day gift us with *Ivan's Childhood, Andrei Rublev, Nostalgia, The Sacrifice*: a body of cinematic masterpieces. On the birthday of Andrei Tarkovsky, we celebrate both him and his father.

05 APRIL

Michigan, 1991. Little Jesse keeping up.

06 APRIL

Jesse before Rome's Pantheon, the burial place of Raphael, the
youthful Renaissance master who died on his thirty-seventh
birthday. Known for his beauty in countenance and spirit, it
was said that Nature wanted him for herself.

07 APRIL

The last painting of Raphael, depicting the Transfiguration,
the alchemized Messiah.

08 APRIL

St. Michael and All Angels Churchyard, East Sussex.
The poet Oliver Ray in close proximity to the unquiet grave.

09 APRIL

Charles Baudelaire was born today in 1821. He believed that
genius was childhood recovered at will. This belief carried
him through his darkest hours, when he dipped his pen into
an inkwell yet another time.

10 APRIL

This palm, woven in Barcelona, represents Jesus' entrance into
Jerusalem, where the people lay their cloaks and palms on the
path before him. Jesus knows what lies ahead, accepting a
brief moment of triumph, comprehending the consequences.

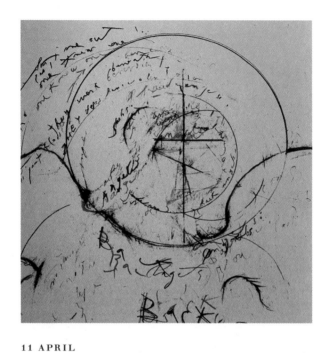

11 APRIL

Drawing energy, channeling the path of Andrei Rublev.

12 APRIL

Sam reading Beckett. Midway, Kentucky.

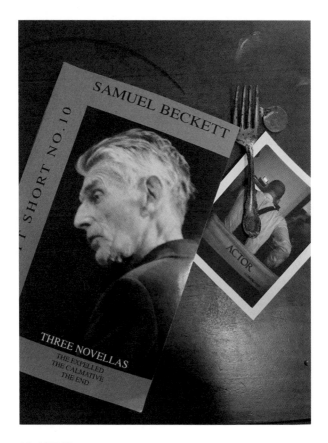

13 APRIL

Samuel Beckett, the great Irish playwright, was born in 1906 on Friday the thirteenth. He was Sam Shepard's literary hero. Sam would recite whole passages of Beckett's work by heart. We often quoted his line "I can't go on, I'll go on." No matter the circumstances, it always made us laugh.

14 APRIL

Anne Sullivan, the American teacher who led young
Helen Keller out of the darkness. On her birthday, we mark
with gratitude the generosity and sacrifices of our teachers.

15 APRIL

Good Friday, Recoleta Cemetery, Buenos Aires.

16 APRIL

Though her transient life was one of sacrifice and physical suffering, Bernadette Soubirous, a peasant girl from Lourdes, had a vision in a grotto that manifested as a healing spring that strengthened the faith of others.

17 APRIL

He is risen. Drawing of the Mystic Lamb by e.g. walker.

18 APRIL

Jean Genet, poet, dramatist, author, and activist, died in Paris
but was laid to rest in an old Spanish cemetery by the sea in
Larache, Tanger-Tetouan-Al Hoceima. He is surrounded by
the scent of wild flowers, stinging salt, and the laughter
of children.

19 APRIL

By the poet's grave, the child Ayoub handed me a silk rose.
A small miracle.

20 APRIL

Uluru. The formation of dreams.

21 APRIL

Privileged to touch its sacred skin.

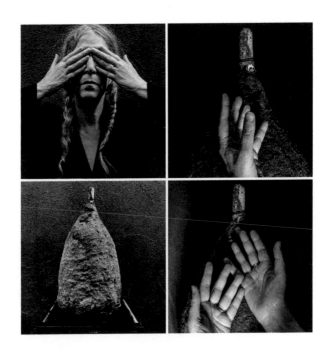

22 APRIL

Earth Day.

SUPPLICATION TO NATURE

If we be blind, if we turn away from Nature, garden of the soul,
She will turn on us. In place of songbird, the shrill cry
of the locusts devouring the harvest, the terrible crackling
of the blazing rainforest, the peatlands smoldering, the seas rising,
cathedrals flooding, the Arctic shelf melting, the Siberian
wood burning, the Barrier Reef bleached as the bones
of forgotten saints. If we be blind, failing in
our supplication to Nature, species will die, the bee
and the butterfly driven to extinction.
All of Nature nothing more than an empty
husk, the unholy ghost of an abandoned
hive.

23 APRIL

A small corner of treasured things. My father's cup, my
Ethiopian cross, Sam's knife, the Libertine's ring.

24 APRIL

The Ethiopian ceremonial cross represents everlasting life and
contains within it an elaborate latticework, an intricate world
of small consonant systems.

25 APRIL

Paris. Jack's Hotel, in the thirteenth arrondissement. Jean
Genet died here, in a small room on the second floor, on April
15, 1986. Suffering with throat cancer, he spent his last days
correcting the galleys of *Prisoner of Love*.

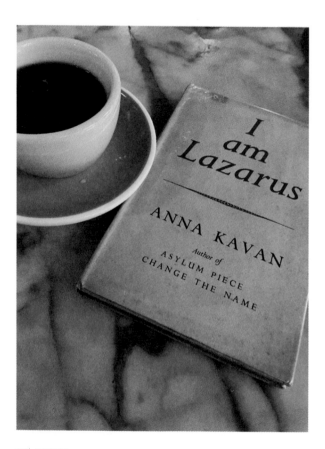

26 APRIL

Coffee and Anna Kavan, on the birthday of the
enigmatic e.g. walker.

27 APRIL

Mexico City. The clock on the wall of Café La Habana,
where the Savage Detectives used to meet, spar, write, and
drink mescal.

28 APRIL

This is the birthday of the Chilean poet and writer
Roberto Bolaño. At the end of his fleeting life, he sat
upon this chair, threw a net over the twentieth century,
and articulated its degeneration in *2666*, the first
masterpiece of the new millennium.

29 APRIL

These days some plans are made optimistically, knowing
they have a great percentage of not happening. Yet the
Imagination reigns. In that respect we can go anywhere,
save by the plot of doubt.

30 APRIL

1951. Germantown, Pennsylvania. An image of pure
happiness—my first bicycle. In my Easter coat, ready to ride
off into the world.

MAY

01 MAY

When I was young, May Day was also called children's day, a time of ribbons and white dresses, turning in circles in the bright fields and fashioning garlands of wildflowers.

02 MAY

In the garden of Pinacoteca Comunale Tacchi-Venturi, a
small but wondrous museum harboring the slippers of
St. Celestine. I have visited many times, due to my affection
for the *Putto with Dolphin* by Andrea del Verrocchio, set
upon a modest fountain.

03 MAY

The *putto*, or cherub, is renowned for its spiral design,
where all angles have equal significance. But it is his
empathetic little face that continues to touch me deeply
and draws me to return.

04 MAY

I am grateful for seemingly small things, as my glasses,
without which I could not read.

05 MAY

The bookcase by my bed, each volume a journey.

06 MAY

In my travels I chanced upon this laundry basket in an alcove
at Egeskov Castle, Denmark. The light was exquisite and the
basket evoked memories of my mother hanging sheets on a
line to dry in the sun.

07 MAY

This is my mother's key ring. The *B* is for Beverly.
She always carried it in the pocket of her housecoat.

08 MAY

Happy Mother's Day to all mothers, holding keys to their
children's hearts.

09 MAY

J. M. Barrie was small for his age but distinguished himself
as a remarkable storyteller. In adulthood he gave us the
monumental *Peter Pan*. Barrie commissioned this statue in
Kensington Gardens, where Peter had his first adventures. It
is often surrounded by lively children eager to fly.

10 MAY

This sculpture in my garden of a boy with birds reminds me of one of the Lost Boys of Neverland. I imagine the bronze birds taking wing when no one is around to hinder potential magic.

11 MAY

Seneca Sebring and his father made me this little birdhouse
for my bungalow. Perhaps one day I will find a tiny bronze
nestling within.

12 MAY

Coffee in Zurich on the artist's birthday.

13 MAY

This is the felt suit of Joseph Beuys, hanging on the wall of a gallery in Zurich. I took a Polaroid and slipped it into my pocket. Later I unpeeled it, revealing the suit of an artist whose work was his activism.

14 MAY

Bolshaya Sadovaya ulitsa no. 10, Moscow, where Mikhail
Bulgakov created his satanic Professor Woland, anonymously
sketched on the stairwell wall.

15 MAY

Mikhail Bulgakov, born this day in Kyiv, in 1891.
He gifted humanity with a true masterpiece, *The Master
and Margarita*, which includes the immortal statement
"Manuscripts don't burn."

16 MAY

A city of burning days and consecrated nights, utterly transformed from the New York I once knew. And yet, somehow it is still my city.

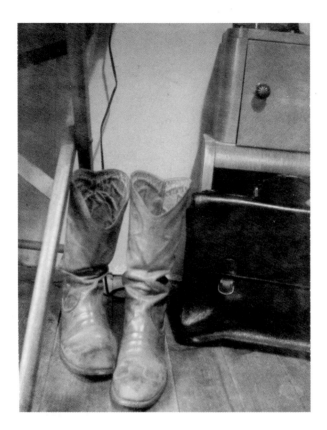

17 MAY

My old Italian cowboy boots experienced much tramping
about until the soles wore through. One evening they seemed
to be urging me to abandon my work and take off again. I put
them on, sat at my desk, and wrote through the night,
adventure enough.

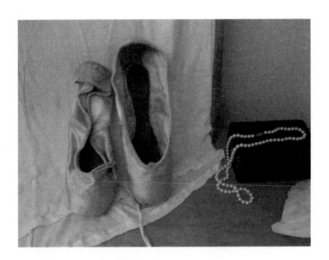

18 MAY

Margot Fonteyn's slippers. A string of pearls from my husband
for my fortieth birthday.

19 MAY

Each day I remind myself how fortunate I am to be the master
of my own ship, with the sustenance to prevail.

20 MAY

The foot pedals of resonant mastery: a dissonant monsoon,
a cacophonic cathedral, the sounds of a weeping heart.

21 MAY

This is the Fender Jazzmaster of Kevin Shields, born
on this day, who founded the deafeningly beautiful
My Bloody Valentine.

22 MAY

Happy birthday, Steven Sebring, intuitive visionary.

23 MAY

Born in Odessa, Anna Akhmatova was one of Russia's most
significant and courageous poets. Banned by the Stalin regime,
surrounded by murderous purging, she chronicled the terrors
gripping the people. In the center of her trials her splendid
poems also reflect an insatiable desire for passionate and
devotional love.

24 MAY

New York City, 1971. Masked in honor of the purveyor of
masks. Happy birthday, Bob Dylan.

have you seen
dylans dog
its got wings
it can fly
if you speak
of it to him
its the only time
dylan
cant look you in the eye

have you held dylans snake
it rattles/like a toy
it coils in his hand
it sleeps in the ~~seed~~   he sleeps in the grass
dylans bed   he's the only one
its the only one   ~~it~~ who ~~not~~
sleeps near his head   when dylan comes

have you pressed
to your ~~soul~~ face
dylans bird dylans bird
it rolls on the ground   it rests on dylans hip
it sings dylans songs   it drops on dylans ground
its the one   it rolls with him
who can hum like dylan hums   its the only one
                                   who can hum when dylan hums

have you seen
dylans dog   it trembles with him
its got wings
it can fly   it rests in dylans hump
then it lands   it trembles inside of him
like a clown   it drops upon the ground
its the only thing allowed   its the only one
look him in the eye   who can hum when dylan hums

goodnight irene.

151

25 MAY

In the Spring of 1971, at the Chelsea Hotel, Sam Shepard and
I dreamt about Bob Dylan. That afternoon I wrote the lyrics to
"Dog Dream." A Dylan lullaby.

26 MAY

New York City, 1976. Strolling Sixth Avenue with pianist
Richard Sohl, born on this day, and the painter Carl
Apfelschnitt. Both gifted men died only days apart, far too
young. As co-founder of the Patti Smith Group, inimitable
accompanist and cherished friend, Richard remains with
us always.

27 MAY

Cowboys and gardenias, the power of the dog.

28 MAY

A corner of my workspace, content in New York light.

29 MAY

In the gray case is the harmonica of a quiet man, devoted
musician, and writer, Tony "Little Sun" Glover. There is also
a yellowed slip of paper inside identifying it as "old leaky."
Given to me by his wife, it is thrice beloved.

30 MAY

On Memorial Day we remember the sacrifice of soldiers. In Rouen the scattered ashes of a country girl who fought to save France. In Verdun a sea of white crosses. Each commemorates a soldier, once a boy racing across the fields.

31 MAY

Jesse reading *Leaves of Grass* at Harleigh Cemetery in
Camden, New Jersey. Walt Whitman heralded the multitude
within us, projecting love and encouragement to future
generations of young poets.

JUNE

01 JUNE

The artist June Leaf, at her Whitney exhibit *Thought Is Infinite*, with her husband, photographer Robert Frank. Both fiercely independent yet of one mind.

02 JUNE

Allen Ginsberg in Washington Square Park, 1966,
serving poetry as if it were bread.

03 JUNE

Commemorating the great poet, activist, and friend on the day of his birth.

04 JUNE

On June 4, 1937, within his atelier at 7 rue des Grands
Augustins, Pablo Picasso completed the masterpiece
Guernica, his statement against war, Fascism, and its
ensuing inhumanity.

05 JUNE

It took several hours for Franco's aerial bombing to destroy
the Basque town of Guernica. Picasso labored for thirty-five
days to paint his response. Art and war, requiring a lifetime
of examination.

06 JUNE

On the Left Bank, steps from the Seine and Notre-Dame
Cathedral, is the treasured bookstore that has tended to writers
and book lovers for over seventy years. There are even a few
cots available for weary poets.

07 JUNE

Through the heart of Paris flows the River Seine, where artists, lovers, and the remains of a burning cathedral are reflected in its currents.

08 JUNE

A boy builds his ship. Diaz Point, Namibia.

09 JUNE

Aboard the *Vajoliroja*, San Juan. A Gemini dreams.

10 JUNE

Mourning architecture,
Notre-Dame Cathedral,
June 2019.

11 JUNE

In the cathedral's interior is this statue of Joan of Arc.
I could not help but wonder if the statue survived the flames,
unlike her namesake.

12 JUNE

Candles lit in memory of the departed in the Abbey of
Saint-Germain-des-Prés.

13 JUNE

The great Japanese writer Osamu Dazai was a self-described aristocratic tramp, yet he wrote with the forbearance of a fasting scribe. He took his own life, his soul flickering on the pages of *No Longer Human*.

14 JUNE

Banzai! Banzai! It is better to write than die.

15 JUNE

This is my late brother, Todd. He loved the Round Table and he was our knight. Happy birthday, heart of my heart.

16 JUNE

Bust of Apollo, Tolstoy House, Moscow.

17 JUNE

I admired her dress. Origin forgotten.

18 JUNE

Coat hanger. Hôtel Bel Ami, Paris.

BY THE PRESIDENT OF THE UNITED STATES OF AMERICA.

A Proclamation.

Whereas, on the twenty-second day of September, in the year of our Lord one thousand eight hundred and sixty-two, a proclamation was issued by the President of the United States, containing, among other things, the following, to wit:

[...]

19 JUNE

Today is Juneteenth. May those who suffered the inhumanity of slavery be solemnly remembered on this day of jubilant celebration.

20 JUNE

Eric Dolphy's musical compositions were multifaceted and
enthralling. He left us too soon, as young prophets often do.

21 JUNE

Listening to "Something Cool" sung by the blond and silky
June Christy, who passed away on the Summer Solstice.

Son of Bamboo presents
Patti Smith Group

Sonic's Rendezvous Band

Masonic Aud.– Detroit
Sat., June 30   8 p.m.
Tickets $8.50 / $9.50

22 JUNE

This slightly tattered flyer announced a memorable concert: my band and Fred's Sonic's Rendezvous. Our amplifiers were loud; Fred, Richard, and Ivan Král were alive; and anything seemed possible.

23 JUNE

Cross-legged on a hill with a book in hand, a statue of
James Joyce watches over his family plot in Zurich's serene
Fluntern Cemetery.

24 JUNE

I thought of Johanna Spyri, writing *Heidi*. I thought of
Joyce, the birth of Dada, and the Cabaret Voltaire. I thought
of Robert Walser walking straight to his end into the
Christmas snow.

25 JUNE

Jesse strolling on a street in Verona.

26 JUNE

Paris, Saint-Germain-des-Prés. The thoroughly modern poet
Guillaume Apollinaire died in 1918, during the Spanish flu
epidemic. In 1959, Picasso offered a bust of the artist Dora
Maar to commemorate the poet. One can easily see the face
of Apollinaire transmuted onto the bronze contours of the
magnificent head.

27 JUNE

My daughter in Rome, so self-contained and otherworldly,
yet deeply connected with the imperative needs of Nature.
Happy birthday, Jesse Paris Smith.

28 JUNE

The photographer Lynn Davis, born on this day, gifted me
with this image of a majestic torso of ice, an aspect of Nature
tragically uncertain.

29 JUNE

This is Snowy, remembered for all the qualities written
above her.

30 JUNE

Jesse's godmother, the artist Patti Hudson, whose ever-present goodness is revealed in her smile. Happy birthday, Patti, we love your snowy soul.

JULY

01 JULY

Everything in my ragged garden is wild.

02 JULY

In honor of the birthday of Hermann Hesse, this is the Smith
Premier No. 4 typewriter on which he wrote his masterpiece
The Glass Bead Game.

03 JULY

A café in Prague by the Charles Bridge, lucidly dreaming of
the writer Franz Kafka on his birthday.

194

04 JULY

Celebrating the freedom to present work on the streets of New York City—a Polaroid of a detail of the Declaration of Independence, adopted on July 4, 1776.

05 JULY

My brother's Navy flag. Bound by him, it will remain ever so in his memory.

06 JULY

Frida Kahlo's birthday. Though often confined to her bed,
her revolutionary heart could not be stilled.

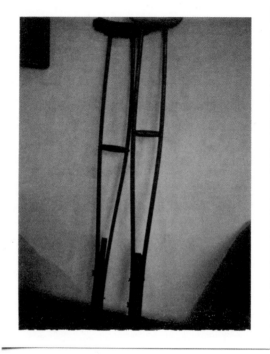

0 7 J U L Y

La Casa Azul, Coyoacán. Frida's crutches. The ground
shook where she stepped.

08 JULY

Limenitis arthemis astyanax, expiring in Midland, Kentucky.

09 JULY

Do you know we exist?
    —JIM MORRISON

The scream of the butterfly, silenced in Paris, July 1971.

10 JULY

Marcel Proust embodied memory in the thousands of pages
written by hand in his sickbed.

11 JULY

The young French detective solving the riddle of lost time.

12 JULY

Susan Sontag's resting place in Montparnasse Cemetery;
the polished surface of her headstone reflecting trees and sky.

13 JULY

Susan had a vast, well-ordered library. She suggested that I acquaint myself with Austrian literature and led me to a section that included Joseph Roth, Robert Musil, Thomas Bernhard, and Hermann Broch. I chose Broch and happily fell under the spell of his incantations of Virgil.

14 JULY

On Bastille Day in 1916, founder of the Dada movement,
Hugo Ball, delivered his manifesto—"Dada is the world soul,
Dada is the pawnshop."

15 JULY

The mummified cat unwittingly left to starve in Joan Miró's
Mallorca studio. A disquieting relic of neglect and remorse.

16 JULY

St. Francis, canonized on this day, watching over my kitchen.

17 JULY

Luc Dietrich's portrait of René Daumal was taken in Paris
during the Second World War, days before the mystic writer
died of consumption. Though Daumal's manuscript *Mount
Analogue* was left unfinished, his last unbridled sentences
possess the spirit of his racing mind.

18 JULY

Nelson Rolihlahla Mandela. Once a young boxer, he rose
as Madiba, the voice of reconciliation, the voice of love.

19 JULY

Triumphal Square, Moscow. On his birthday, consider the work
of Vladimir Mayakovsky, who possessed the air of both a poet
and a thug, gifting us with poetry as revolutionary as himself.

20 JULY

Within the course of *Blade Runner*, Rutger Hauer infused his own humanity into Roy Batty's android heart. Remembering the actor, imbued with Batty's powers, sailing off the shoulder of Orion, seeing things we humans would not believe.

21 JULY

Struggle.

22 JULY

Trutnov, Czech Republic. Sometimes the world seems nuts.

23 JULY

A lot to think about.

24 JULY

Jejenji, a temple in Osaka. The incense burner one lights
when paying respects to the great Japanese writer Ryūnosuke
Akutagawa, creator of *Rashomon*. Fearing madness, seeking
peace, he took his life on this day.

25 JULY

As the smoke rises, one can envision him contemplating his
sacred objects, words spreading like an ancient spell.

26 JULY

Sam's Adirondack chairs in Kentucky. We would drink our coffee, talk about writing, or just watch the sun go down in comfortable silence.

27 JULY

On his passing day, Sam Shepard's Stetson.

28 JULY

The Lion of Lucerne, mortally wounded, dreaming of his pride.

29 JULY

Mantua, New Jersey, 1982. My father used to say that life is like golf. Just when you want to toss the clubs, there's a birdie or a hole in one to draw you back in. Happy birthday, Daddy, may eagles abound.

30 JULY

Emily Brontë, mirroring her own restive soul, immortalized
the ghosts haunting the moors that she often roamed with her
loyal mastiff Keeper.

31 JULY

My same wild garden. Life everywhere.

AUGUST

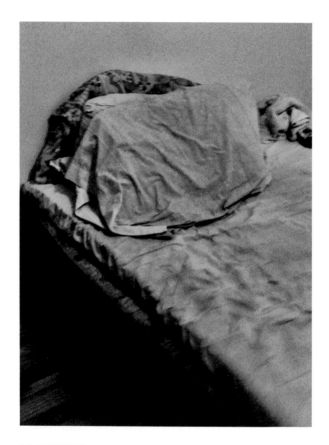

223

01 AUGUST

Jim Carroll's bed. Remembering the poet and performer on his birthday, a date shared with Herman Melville and Jerry Garcia; beautiful dreamers.

02 AUGUST

Bellefontaine Cemetery, St. Louis. The modest headstone
of the beloved and infamous father of the beats is beside the
monument erected to his grandfather and namesake, William
Seward Burroughs, inventor of the adding machine.

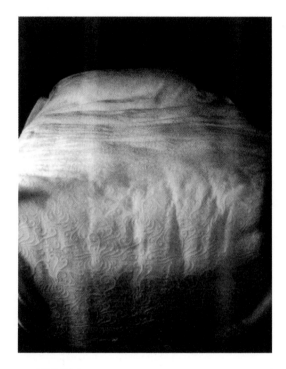

03 AUGUST

Wentworth Place, North London. The sickbed of the poet
John Keats. The atmosphere seems to contain the luminous
dust of his consumptive nights.

04 AUGUST

In the Cimitero Protestante, Rome, not far from the grave of
Keats, lies the poet Percy Bysshe Shelley. On the morning of
his birthday, focusing my lens, his restless spirit seemed to rise
and enter the frame.

05 AUGUST

Born on this day, my son, Jackson Frederick Smith,
the family's protector and joy.

06 AUGUST

Ghostly witness: Atomic Bomb Dome. The only structure that
withstood the catastrophic devastation of the atomic bomb
dropped on Hiroshima at the end of World War II. A chorus of
voices rise: Remember humanity, all else is dust.

BOMB

Budger of history   Brake of time   You   Bomb
Toy of universe   Grandest of all snatched-sky   I cannot hate you
Do I hate the mischievous thunderbolt   the jawbone of an ass
The bumpy club of One Million B.C.   the mace   the flail   the axe
Catapult Da Vinci   tomahawk Cochise   flintlock Kidd   dagger Rathbone
Ah and the sad desperate gun of Verlaine   Pushkin   Dillinger   Bogart
And hath not St. Michael a burning sword   St. George a lance   David a sling
Bomb   you are as cruel as man makes you   and you're no crueller than cancer
All man hates you   they'd rather die by car-crash   lightning   drowning
Falling off a roof   electric-chair   heart-attack   old age   old age   O Bomb
They'd rather die by anything but you   Death's finger is free-lance
Not up to man whether you boom or not   Death has long since distributed its
categorical blue   I sing thee Bomb   Death's extravagance   Death's jubilee
Gem of Death's supremest blue   The flyer will crash   his death will differ
with the climber who'll fall   To die by cobra is not to die by bad pork
Some die by swamp   some by sea   and some by the bushy-haired man in the night
O there are deaths like witches of Arc   Scarey deaths like Boris Karloff
No-feeling deaths like birth-death   sadless deaths like old pain Bowery
Abandoned deaths   like Capital Punishment   stately deaths like senators
And unthinkable deaths like Harpo Marx   girls on Vogue covers   my own
I do not know just how horrible Bombdeath is   I can only imagine
Yet no other death I know has so laughable a preview   I scope
a city   New York City   streaming   starkeyed   subway shelter
Scores and scores   A fumble of humanity   High heels bend
Hats whelming away   Youth forgetting their combs
Ladies not knowing what to do   with their shopping bags
Unperturbed gum machines   Yet dangerous 3rd rail
Ritz Brothers   from the Bronx   caught in the A train
The smiling Schenley poster will always smile
Impish Death   Satyr Bomb   Bombdeath
Turtles exploding over Istanbul
The jaguar's flying foot
soon to sink in arctic snow
Penguins plunged against the Sphinx
The top of the Empire State
arrowed in a broccoli field in Sicily
Eiffel shaped like a C in Magnolia Gardens
St. Sophia peeling over Sudan
O athletic Death   Sportive Bomb
The temples of ancient times
their grand ruin ceased
Electrons   Protons   Neutrons
gathering Hesperean hair
walking the dolorous golf of Arcady
joining marble helmsmen
entering the final amphitheater
with a hymnody feeling of all Troys
heralding cypressean torches
racing plumes and banners
and yet knowing Homer with a step of grace

07 AUGUST

Gregory Corso was the youngest and most provocative of the beats. His mocking embrace of the bomb, in his lengthy and controversial poem, was often misunderstood, as was he and the best minds of his generation.

GREGORY CORSO
POETA
26·3·1930 → 17·1·2001
Spirt
is Life
It flows thru
the death of
endlessly
like a river
unafraid
of becoming
the sea

08 AUGUST

Gregory loved the Romantic poets. He is buried at the foot of Shelley, though in karmic keeping with Gregory's mischievous ways, the word spirit is misspelled on his headstone.

09 AUGUST

On Jerry Garcia's passing day, I sit in my favorite chair, listen
to the Grateful Dead. *Look out of any window, any morning,
any evening, any day.*

10 AUGUST

The abstract expressionist painter Lee Krasner is buried at the
Green River Cemetery, Springs, New York. Years before,
husband Jackson Pollock unearthed a massive stone in Springs
as a possible sculptural element. That stone now marks her
grave, a perfect union.

11 AUGUST

Krasner chose the commanding boulder that marks the grave
of Pollock, one of the most important artists of the twentieth
century. Moss and lichen spatter the surface; Nature's homage
to the drips and tendrils of his furious process.

12 AUGUST

This photograph of Jackson Pollock and Lee Krasner by
Hans Namuth was given to me by my husband. It hung in the
kitchen of our Michigan home, our common guides.

BLUE POLES

Mother as I write the sun dissolves
Blood life streaming cross my hand
And these words, these words
Hope dashed immortal hope
Hope streaking the canvas sky
Blue poles infinitely winding, as I write, as I write
Blue poles infinitely winding, as I write, as I write

We joined the long caravan
Hungry dreaming going west

We buried him by the river
Blue poles infinitely winding, as I write, as I write
Blue poles infinitely winding, as I write, I write

235

13 AUGUST

The song "Blue Poles" takes its title from one of Pollock's greatest paintings. The lyrics speak of the hardships faced in the Great Depression; a metaphor for the personal struggles of Krasner and Pollock, and perhaps something of our own.

14 AUGUST

The effigy of a humble fisherman with his net, surrounded by gulls, stands before the Oslo city hall.

15 AUGUST

Gustave Doré illustrated the visionary poet Samuel Coleridge's masterpiece *The Rime of the Ancient Mariner*. It recounts the tribulations of an accursed sailor whose arrow pierced the heart of a benevolent albatross.

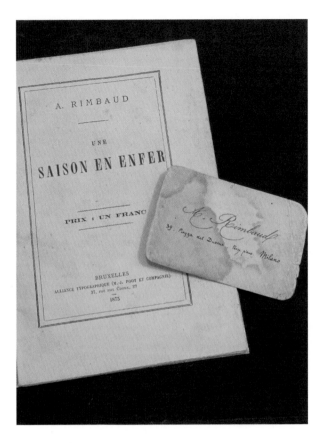

16 AUGUST

In August 1873, wrestling his own demons, Arthur Rimbaud
completed *A Season in Hell.* This is his self-published edition
and his calling card, of which only three exist.

17 AUGUST

In the Pavillon de la Reine hotel, where one can dream
beneath a faithful facsimile of Rimbaud's manuscript. Strange
though breathtaking, one can trace the curves of each word,
miraculous and embittered.

18 AUGUST

Enid Starkie was a brilliant Irish scholar whose biography of Rimbaud was the first to map his pursuits in East Africa and capture the mythic atmosphere of his too short life. On her birthday, I recall how much the fruits of her tireless research meant to me as a young reader.

19 AUGUST

Two treasured books, written by Starkie. I found them on a dusty shelf in the Strand Book Store, where I worked in the basement in the Summer of 1973.

20 AUGUST

H. P. Lovecraft, the father of cosmic horror, born on this day, was a complex, twisted genius who died in the shadows, poverty stricken. His dark paranoia aside, the Cthulhu Mythos has captivated and inspired generations of science fiction writers in search of alternate universes.

21 AUGUST

The Burroughs calculating machine, patented August 21, 1888,
is flanked by his grandson William's worn bandana.

22 AUGUST

This poignant sculpture of Hagar, an Egyptian
slave, was carved by the celebrated Black sculptor
Edmonia Lewis. Hagar was unjustly exiled in the
desert with her child, Ishmael. She was led to water
by an angel because she called to God, surrendering
yet magnifying herself.

23 AUGUST

Michael Stipe's portrait of sleep.
Rest in peace, River Phoenix.
August 23, 1970–October 31, 1993.

24 AUGUST

Simone Weil, French philosopher and political activist, was
a numinous soul who sought the core of truth. She fled her
beloved France due to religious persecution, suffered
consumption and was laid to rest in Ashford, England.
Albert Camus championed her, publishing her transcendent
works *Gravity and Grace* and *The Working Condition*,
rescuing her from obscurity.

25 AUGUST

La Roche-en-Ardenne. A path is created. Curious, we follow
with this rhyme in our pocket: *One road is paved in gold, one
road is just a road.*

26 AUGUST

Jimi Hendrix opened his Electric Lady Studios on this day in
1970. It was his hope to write, record, and collaborate with
musicians all over the world, drawing from a collective sonic
chaos a harmonic language of peace. Tragically, Jimi died in
London three weeks later, bequeathing his vision to the future.

27 AUGUST

In 1976, *Horses,* recorded at Electric Lady Studios, received the Grand Prix du Disque, the premier French recording award. Lenny Kaye and I proudly accepted it in Paris.

28 AUGUST

The birthday of the multi-disciplined German poet Johann Wolfgang von Goethe. He gave us *Faust*, *The Sorrows of Young Werther*, *The Metamorphosis of Plants*, and *Theory of Colours*. Great works inspire, the rest is up to us.

29 AUGUST

A humble stone table in Jena, in the garden of Friedrich Schiller. Around it, Goethe, Schiller, and Alexander von Humboldt would share philosophical visions and thoughts on the nature of the cosmos. The ginkgo leaf is from a tree in the garden, said to have regenerated from one that Goethe had planted.

30 AUGUST

Mary Shelley, born on this day, penned her masterpiece,
Frankenstein; or, The Modern Prometheus, at the age of
eighteen. Drawing from her imagination and the atmosphere
of her time, she created the most complex monster in
literature, the Creature who quoted Coleridge and mourned
his own hideousness.

31 AUGUST

Two little pals on my bureau discussing how to stitch the
world back together again.

SEPTEMBER

255

01 SEPTEMBER

Coney Island, September 1, 1969. On our second anniversary,
Robert Mapplethorpe and I celebrated the beginning of a
new life in New York City.

02 SEPTEMBER

Wishing a worthy fellow a happy birthday.

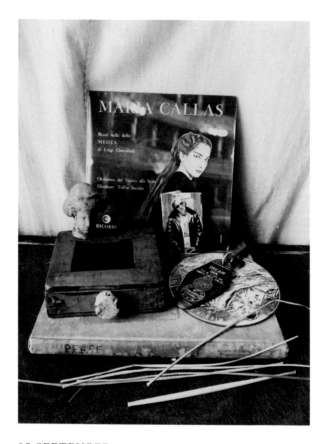

03 SEPTEMBER

A tableau for the late Sandy Pearlman, producer, lyricist,
creator of *The Soft Doctrines of Imaginos*. He loved *Medea*
and *The Matrix*, Maria Callas and rock and roll. A maestro of
spiritual proximities.

04 SEPTEMBER

These leather booties, so small they fit in the palm of the hand, were worn by Antonin Artaud, the deeply complex and influential French writer, poet, dramatist, and actor, born in Marseille on this day in 1896.

Ivry
in a room like any other.
in a room like no other
in this solitary cell
clouded with light
on this tinsel pavilion
propped with deep souls
sits a sleeping friend
the burgeoning flowers
the principal
within the hollow
the excitement
of divine sorrow
buds and shoots
still where he sits.
posing as sleeping.
but he is not sleeping
The twisted sheets
hands like vines
extend into shadow
at the foot of the bed
at the comic foot
in the room –
the nerve center .
a green chair
by the dresser
a boot of cloth
white shirting
a dressing gown
a breathing shroud
at the foot of the bed
the comic foot

The truce that bridges
all those twilight journeys   [NO FILM
The white bars   [MIRROR.)
in the room like
nothing
in the comic
stillness
with his hands all
folded
in this lovely journey
on this lovely morning
bonds of laughter
glories
and the vines
all twisting
and the vines
like sheeting .
the light straining
the dangling
at the foot of the bed
still where he sits
straining
at the foot of the bed
the comic foot
another step
like no other
past the green chair
the dresser
from this room
like any other
the light stained
feet
toward the twisted sleep
where deep souls walk
in Ivry
where it's morning

05 SEPTEMBER

Artaud died at the foot of his bed in a psychiatric clinic in Ivry-sur-Seine. This poem imagines his final steps from the confines of an asylum toward an unfathomed freedom.

06 SEPTEMBER

My old traveling boots. Time to get moving.

07 SEPTEMBER

Cairo always knows when I am getting ready to leave.

08 SEPTEMBER

A Moscow suburb is the home of the great Russian novelist
Leo Tolstoy. At the bottom of the stairs a stately bear holds a
small silver plate, where visitors left their calling cards.
Often Tolstoy could not be found, as he spent much time
roaming in the woods.

09 SEPTEMBER

Tolstoy was born on this day. He gave us *War and Peace*, *Anna Karenina*, and *The Kingdom of God Is Within You*. He imprinted the concept of universal love and pacifism through his towering contribution to literature.

10 SEPTEMBER

A dove from my father's collection of porcelain birds, a symbol
of devotion and peace.

11 SEPTEMBER

September 11, 2001. South Tower. Mixed media, gold.
We bend to remember the departed, then rise to embrace
the living.

12 SEPTEMBER

There is the promise of morning.

13 SEPTEMBER

Big Sur, cosmic debris.

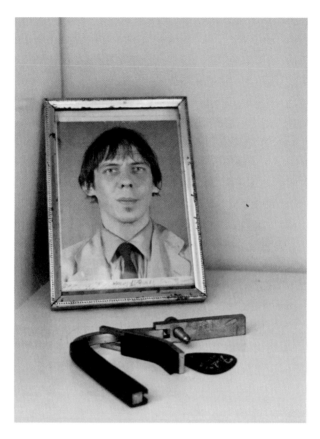

14 SEPTEMBER

Fred Sonic Smith.
September 14, 1948–November 4, 1994.
Memory is Music.

15 SEPTEMBER

This is Fred's Mosrite, the guitar that served our
cultural revolution. No hands save his have played it.

16 SEPTEMBER

Thessaloniki, Greece. Hats off to good men.

17 SEPTEMBER

The highly influential American singer-songwriter Hank
Williams recorded fifty-five singles in his brief, tumultuous
life. "Lovesick Blues," "Your Cheatin' Heart," and "I'm So
Lonesome I Could Cry," to name a few. Happy birthday, Hank,
thank you for the songs that we all find ourselves singing.

18 SEPTEMBER

With heaven's dime I would call time past.

19 SEPTEMBER

Remembering Elvis Aaron Presley.
He stepped out of high school, alien, otherworldly, evolving
quickly as the matrix of the burgeoning energy and cultural
shift of the nineteen-fifties.

20 SEPTEMBER

Train station, Brussels.
The contentment of being
on the move, even when
not moving.

21 SEPTEMBER

Richard Wright, whose seminal books on racism in America include *Native Son* and *Black Boy*, also composed haiku. This is his meditation for the Fall Equinox: *This autumn evening / Is full of an empty sky / And one empty road.*

22 SEPTEMBER

Walking down a Paris street on the birthday of Anna Karina, the captivating actress and muse of Jean-Luc Godard, I was drawn to an image of her wielding scissors, her weapon of choice in *Pierrot le Fou*.

23 SEPTEMBER

Musician John Coltrane infused his own spiritual quest in
his evolving compositions; his improvisation a kind of prayer.
The five-part *Meditations* take us to the threshold of a celestial
portal, giving form to the formless, unconstrained yet
palatable, inspirational and divine.

24 SEPTEMBER

Revering Coltrane beyond all others, Fred took up the tenor saxophone. We often improvised together, on sax and clarinet, striving to interpret the paintings of Pollock.

25 SEPTEMBER

San Remo, Italy. A Pythagorean traveler.

26 SEPTEMBER

When I was young, a line from "The Love Song of J. Alfred Prufrock" strangely resonated. *I grow old . . . I grow old . . . I shall wear the bottoms of my trousers rolled.* Decades later, I am happily that person. Happy birthday, T. S. Eliot.

27 SEPTEMBER

The anti-poet Nicanor Parra influenced generations of poets
and revolutionaries. He was cited by Bolaño as the greatest
living poet of the Spanish language. The blissfully irreverent
Parra, winner of the Cervantes Prize, lived to be 103, adhering
to the philosophy that true seriousness resides in the comic.

28 SEPTEMBER

One Fall morning, I found the locked gate left open to Willy's
Memorial Garden, just north of Washington Square Park,
more an alley than a courtyard. There, before a wall of silvery
ivy and inkberries, was a statue of Miguel de Cervantes,
creator of Don Quixote, dreamer of dreams.

29 SEPTEMBER

In Fez, the song of the birds resonated in the tiled halls, sacred music mingled with the language of stars. Happy birthday, Rosemary Carroll, quiet warrior, loyal friend.

30 SEPTEMBER

My mother gave me this likeness of Rumi, revered Sufi mystic and poet. Rumi said that life is the balance of holding on and letting go. In the night, I imagine the little statue turning in silent adoration.

OCTOBER

287

01 OCTOBER

The artist James Lee Byars created *The Sphere of Generosity*, an imperfect ball of handmade clay evoking the perfect sentiment.

02 OCTOBER

The charkha is an ancient Indian spinning wheel, elevated as a symbol for India's political independence, the simple act of spinning an act of protest. "It is in the daily life," wrote Gandhi, "where dharma and practicality come together, and the spinning wheel was the realization of this possibility."

03 OCTOBER

St. Francis of Assisi, patron saint of Nature and her creatures, passed this day in 1226. He died reciting *I cry with my voice to the Lord*, from a psalm of David, in his humble bed, leaving nothing material behind save his threadbare garments.

04 OCTOBER

The acclaimed pianist Glenn Gould was celebrated for his
mastery of Bach, who seemed to possess him. The inhuman
energy in his version of *The Goldberg Variations* was
unprecedented. Roberto Bolaño religiously listened to the
Variations on headphones as he furiously attempted to finish
2666 before his untimely death.

05 OCTOBER

The Swedish author and political activist Henning Mankell
gave us police inspector Kurt Wallander, in a series of complex
mystery novels. Wallander obsessively solves crimes, often
unveiling political corruption while allaying loneliness with
alcohol and Maria Callas. Henning was my friend. The
photograph, taken before he died, captures something of his
august nature.

06 OCTOBER

Hotel Indigo, Bath. The overhead light fixture, a brass atom, spiritedly merging science and design.

07 OCTOBER

Marie Curie's contributions to physics and science helped to reshape our world. Thankfully, she had the will to overcome the barriers facing a young Polish girl in the field of science. Staggering all, she discovered radium and was the recipient of the 1911 Nobel Prize in chemistry, the first woman to receive it. Combined with her courage was her generosity, as she willingly shared her research and financial gain with others.

08 OCTOBER

A.N.S.W.E.R. Rally against war with Iraq, 2002, Washington,
D.C. On the Reverend Jesse Jackson's birthday, we extend
gratitude for his inspirational leadership.

09 OCTOBER

Imagining peace. John Lennon born.

10 OCTOBER

On October 10 and 11, 1963, the citizens of France mourned
the successive deaths of Édith Piaf and Jean Cocteau. The
little sparrow sang her mournful song, calling to the artist.
Hastening to join her, their dual profiles could be traced in the
brightening sky.

11 OCTOBER

Y is the exhausted, inexhaustible force.

12 OCTOBER

In Teotihuacán, near the Avenue of the Dead, a small deity
holds an orb in his two hands.

13 OCTOBER

In a dark corner not far from the Pyramid of the Sun is an ancient wheel, symbolic of the birth of thought.

14 OCTOBER

Backstage at CBGB. A wave and salute to Hilly Kristal and all who have played and passed through its doors.

15 OCTOBER

October 15, 2006, marked the closing of CBGB. My band, joined by Flea, gave the final performance, ending with a eulogy to our departed musicians and friends. The last flowers received were calla lilies, symbolizing innocence and rebirth.

16 OCTOBER

Grant Park, Chicago. Flea, master musician and friend,
practicing Bach runs on his bass at festival grounds.

17 OCTOBER

In 2010 I joined Pete Seeger to benefit ALBA, an organization preserving the history of those who volunteered in the 1930s to fight Fascism in Spain. Seeger was ninety-one, filled with activist energy. His trusty banjo, set by the stage, was tattooed with the words *This machine surrounds hate and forces it to surrender.*

18 OCTOBER

Frank Gehry's masterpiece, the breathtaking Guggenheim
Museum, built of limestone, glass, and steel, and clad with
titanium scales, rises alongside the city's Nervión River, the
estuary of Bilbao, Spain.

19 OCTOBER

Racing through a Richard Serra.

20 OCTOBER

In the Église Saint-Rémi, where Rimbaud's funeral service
was held, is the font where he was baptized. On his birthday,
a woebegone chorus: Even in the thick of things true poets
stand alone.

21 OCTOBER

In 1904, at twenty-seven years of age, Isabelle Eberhardt, writer and explorer, drowned in the desert in a rare flash flood, leaving behind hundreds of handwritten pages to be posthumously published. She wrote *The Oblivion Seekers,* yet sought love, knowledge, and God.

22 OCTOBER

Chuffilly-Roche. The Rimbaud family compound was bombed
in World War I, then rebuilt from the rubble. The house sits
on the same land where they harvested corn and the poet
wrestled with *A Season in Hell*. Having come into my hands, it
touches me to read the plaque attached to the stone façade: *At
this place Rimbaud hoped, despaired, and suffered.*

23 OCTOBER

As guardian of the Rimbaud property, I can freely explore it.
I found an encrusted horseshoe partially buried, a sign of
protection and hopefully one of good work and good luck.

24 OCTOBER

With Christoph Maria Schlingensief in Venice at the home of
Marco Polo. He was a life force, an artist, activist, director, and
filmmaker. Of his death shortly before his fiftieth birthday,
Elfriede Jelinek wrote, "I always thought one like him cannot
die. It is as if life itself had died."

25 OCTOBER

Picasso's *Bust of Sylvette*, LaGuardia Place. Discovering the
work of Picasso as a young girl inspired me to seek new ways
of seeing, propelling me toward the artist's path. Happy
birthday, Pablo Picasso, I never cease to be grateful.

26 OCTOBER

St. Thomas à Becket churchyard, Heptonstall, feels a lonely place. I visit when I am able to spend time at the grave of Sylvia Plath, opening *Ariel* to "Poppies in October"—*A gift, a love gift / Utterly unasked for.*

27 OCTOBER

Lou Reed, ambassador to New York's wild side, departed on
the anniversary of the birth of two of our greatest poets,
Dylan Thomas and Sylvia Plath. I didn't always understand
the intensity of his moods, but I understood Lou's devotion to
poetry and the transporting quality of his performances.

28 OCTOBER

To the North. Oil and paper collage on canvas. Lee Krasner,
great American abstract expressionist painter.

29 OCTOBER

It was my writer's house by the sea, all but destroyed in 2012
when Hurricane Sandy devastated the East Coast. My
neighbors kindly hung a flag upon it to protect it from looting.
The structure remained intact and in time it was refurbished,
my sanctuary.

30 OCTOBER

The artist Joan Mitchell, 73 rue Galande, Paris, 1948.

*"The solitude that I find in my studio is one of plenitude.
I am enough for myself. I live fully there."*

31 OCTOBER

William S. Burroughs. Lawrence, Kansas.

NOVEMBER

01 NOVEMBER

This is my thinking chair. I sit and let it take me where it will, as if it were a small wooden ship, or just watch the light play upon its linen coverlet.

02 NOVEMBER

Pier Paolo Pasolini was a controversial yet celebrated Italian poet and filmmaker whose *Gospel According to St. Matthew* righteously painted Christ as a revolutionary figure. Pasolini was slain in Ostia, Italy, on All Souls' Day. A monument with doves entwined was erected where his body was found, not far from the sea.

03 NOVEMBER

Hotel Majestic, Bologna. On the road I often rinse my T-shirts
in the sink and let them dry by the window in the sun.

04 NOVEMBER

On Robert Mapplethorpe's birthday I think of the ecstatic
sacrifice of artists and the body of work they leave behind.

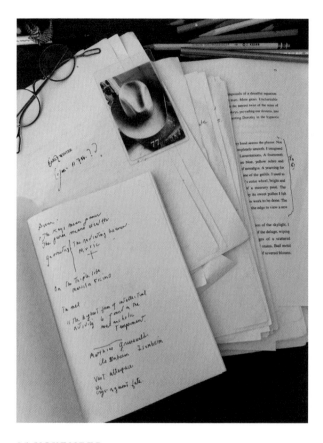

05 NOVEMBER

Sam Shepard and I spent a lot of time talking about his horses, his land, and the writer's laboriously holy process. Thinking of him on his birthday, as I attempt to rein in a manuscript.

06 NOVEMBER

A long stroll in Coyoacán takes one past the former homes
of Frida Kahlo and Leon Trotsky. In the silvery twilight
the intricate palms rival the historic beauty of the
surrounding architecture.

07 NOVEMBER

In a nearby plaza is La Conchita—the little shell—the
oldest European church in Mexico. It is admired for its twin
bell towers and Baroque ornamentation of volcanic stone.
The interior is unadorned, save for the large golden reredos
behind the altar that seems to project a light of its own.

08 NOVEMBER

In the Welsh city of Laugharne, a white horse awaits.

09 NOVEMBER

On a hill by St. Martin's Church, not very far from Laugharne
Castle, where the poet wrote *Portrait of the Artist as a Young
Dog,* a plain wood cross marks the resting place of Dylan
Thomas and his wife, Caitlin. Ascending the hill, I was
greeted by a three-legged dog, said to be a good omen.

10 NOVEMBER

Poet, seer, and solitary adventurer, Arthur Rimbaud was
buried next to his younger sister Vitalie in his birthplace
in Charleville. On the morning of November 10, 1891,
he requested transport on a ship to his adopted home of
Abyssinia. His right leg amputated, he died that afternoon;
his final journey confined to his visionary mind.

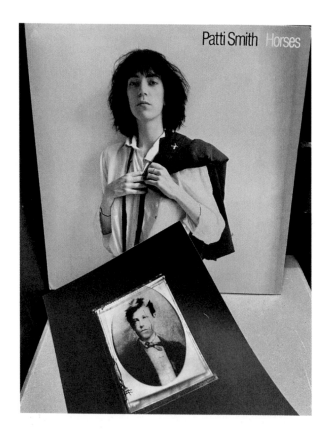

The album *Horses* was to be released on Rimbaud's birthday. Delayed, it was serendipitously released on November 10, 1975, the anniversary of his death. While we recorded, a sense of the transgressive poet permeated the atmosphere, his name invoked in the song "Land," a wild boy's journey.
Go Rimbaud!

11 NOVEMBER

11:11. Make a wish.

12 NOVEMBER

Sor Juana Inés de la Cruz, the Mexican philosopher, composer, poet, and proto-feminist Hieronymite nun, was born on this day. Considering the breadth of this rare being, her words fall as a child's song: *The matter to me was simple/love for you was so strong, I could see you in my soul/ and talk to you all day long.*

13 NOVEMBER

On the birthday of Robert Louis Stevenson, a boy's Thomas the Train and the desire to go anywhere.

14 NOVEMBER

When I was in my twenties, I imagined being published
by Gallimard and visiting their historic garden in Paris, where
some of the greatest minds in French literature could be
found smoking a cigarette or talking philosophy. Now, the
dream realized, I sit in the garden as I like, to share coffee with
the ghosts of Camus and Sartre and Simone de Beauvoir.

15 NOVEMBER

Happy twenty-first birthday, Cairo, my Abyssinian runt.

16 NOVEMBER

This is happily sparring with my girlhood friend Jane Sparks. She seemed much bolder than the rest of us, yet in truth was more vulnerable, good-hearted, leaving all too soon. Remembering Jane's fighting spirit on her birthday.

17 NOVEMBER

Discovering the Austrian writer Marlen Haushofer during lockdown was a revelation. In her novel *The Wall*, the sole survivor of an unnamed global catastrophe deflects self-pity and inspires one to self-motivate and work harder.

18 NOVEMBER

A solitary bird sings of the death of Proust.

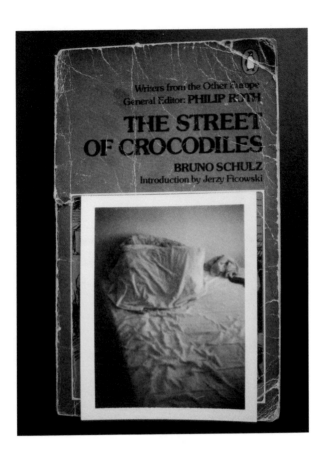

19 NOVEMBER

Bruno Schulz, the brilliant Polish writer, was shot in the street
by a Gestapo officer on this date in 1942. Much of his writing,
including a work called *The Messiah*, was tragically lost in the
war. This is Jim Carroll's heavily thumbed copy of Schulz's
masterpiece *The Street of Crocodiles*.

20 NOVEMBER

In the Galleria Borghese, in Rome, there are two moving depictions of John the Baptist. As a young shepherd boy resting upon his red cloak, painted by Caravaggio, and Giovanni Antonio Houdon's sculpture of the Baptist reaching to touch the head of the Redeemer.

21 NOVEMBER

Our rugged American landscape.

22 NOVEMBER

On this day our president John F. Kennedy was assassinated.
I was sixteen and it was the saddest day of my young life.
Now I am thankful that I am still here to accept the blessed
task of remembrance.

23 NOVEMBER

A family outing in Central Park.

24 NOVEMBER

Thanksgiving. Carlo Collodi, born today, gave us *Pinocchio*.
This wonderful book embodies all that is required in
becoming truly human; personifying William Blake's *Songs
of Innocence and Experience*. I still possess my beloved
and battered copy, given to me by my mother on my
seventh birthday.

25 NOVEMBER

Made from a bundle of bound twigs, this is the broom
that was used to sweep the dying leaves from the grave of
Yukio Mishima.

26 NOVEMBER

This guitar, a Depression-era Gibson given to me by
Sam Shepard, has played a song for Rothko, of a ribbon of
blood, the artist's perfect red.

27 NOVEMBER

Happy birthday, Jimi Hendrix, shaman of our age.

28 NOVEMBER

William Blake was born on this day in 1757. From his window
as a child, Blake perceived the presence of God. As a young
man, he saw choruses of angels in the fields. A transcendent
artist who spoke out against injustice, Blake died in poverty, but
not of the spirit. He remained a prolific visionary, heralding
the meekness of the lamb and the tiger's fearful symmetry.

29 NOVEMBER

Torre del Lago. The piano that Giacomo Puccini composed his greatest operas on. Touching the keys, I felt an unmistakable vibration, recalling the passionate aria "E lucevan le stelle," sung by the artist Cavaradossi awaiting execution. Gazing at the stars, he feels the pulsation of his own blood, an overflowing desire to live.

30 NOVEMBER

A pathway in Padua leads to the Scrovegni Chapel. The
interior of the small fourteenth-century church is covered,
wall to ceiling, with frescoes by Giotto, depicting the life cycle
of Christ and the Virgin. They were created to convey a hope
for human salvation. Exiting, one is suddenly struck by the
work of Nature: innocent sky, leaves of gold.

DECEMBER

01 DECEMBER

Were there only an imagined elixir to heal our friends, our angels. On World AIDS Day we mourn those we have lost as we recommit to protect and educate new generations.

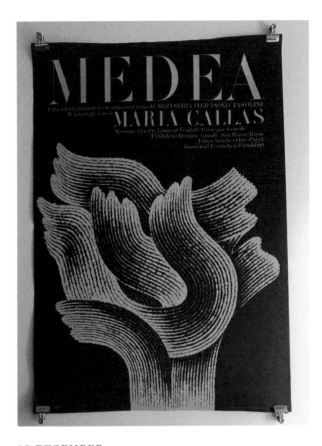

02 DECEMBER

Recognizing the tragic aura of the great soprano, Pasolini cast Maria Callas as his Medea. Although she died alone and broken-hearted, their unique friendship provided her with the warmth of consolation and the opportunity to soar.

03 DECEMBER

Port of Alexandria. Master of montage and breathless
connections. Mastermind of the French New Wave.
Happy birthday to Jean-Luc Godard.

04 DECEMBER

Rosa Parks was arrested on December 1, 1955, when she refused to give up her seat to a white man. This justified act of defiance helped ignite the civil rights movement. Her words are a beacon: "Each person must live their life as a model for others."

05 DECEMBER

Joan Didion. A pure writer.

06 DECEMBER

A guardian at the entrance of the Dorotheenstadt Cemetery in Berlin. Visiting the grave of Bertolt Brecht, I always pause to touch her wings.

07 DECEMBER

La Scala. Opening night, 2007. The opera concluded,
Waltraud Meier hesitates behind the curtain. The great
German mezzo-soprano, covered in the blood of Tristan, still
harboring the soul of Isolde.

08 DECEMBER

Jesse gowned, pauses in the La Scala opera house museum,
Milan. My Maria.

09 DECEMBER

Intermission. Contemplating Puccini's *Tosca*, the favorite lines of an aria, *I have lived for art, for love.*

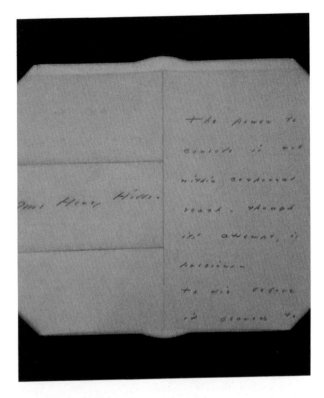

10 DECEMBER

A treasured possession, a letter—small and complex born—
written in the hand of the poet Emily Dickinson.

11 DECEMBER

In her brief life, American chemist Alice Augusta Ball developed the first successful treatment for leprosy. The Ball Method offered hope to those quarantined for life in leper colonies. Although Alice Ball died at the age of twenty-four, she made it possible for the most marginalized in society to return to their families.

12 DECEMBER

The great Japanese film director Yasujiro Ozu, who gave us classics such as *Tokyo Story* and *Late Spring,* with Setsuko Hara in lead roles, died on his sixtieth birthday. His headstone bears the single character *mu,* which signifies nothingness.

13 DECEMBER

The expressive face of Setsuko Hara dominated six of Ozu's
celebrated films. She quietly withdrew from films not long
after Ozu's death, living reclusively for the next half century.
When I visited the grave of Ozu, I found her resting place a
few meters away from his, white chrysanthemums at the foot.

14 DECEMBER

The painting *Repose* by Édouard Manet is an incandescent
study of the artist and muse Berthe Morisot, who through
great determination developed her own body of work and held
her own among the giants of impressionism.

15 DECEMBER

Gerhard Richter's clouds, fractured harbingers of change.

16 DECEMBER

In 1302, Dante Alighieri was exiled from Florence, and found protection in Ravenna, where he wrote *The Divine Comedy*. This memorial marks the site where benevolent monks hid the poet's remains from the Nazis, guarding them with their life, as their predecessors had done for centuries.

17 DECEMBER

The citizens of Florence, regretting the expulsion of Dante, erected an imposing statue in his honor.

18 DECEMBER

Albertine Sarrazin, petite saint of maverick writers. Born in
Algiers, abandoned and abused, she worked the Paris streets,
did time for robbery, and assembled her prison arsenal:
Gauloises, black coffee, and eyebrow pencil. A life cut short,
she left works that fuse the bone of art and life.

19 DECEMBER

The writings of Jean Genet were banned in America until
1964. On his birthday, we celebrate the freedom to obtain and
read his body of work and regard the master who drove thorns
of love and theft deep into the heart of poetry.

20 DECEMBER

Hive Eye and Winghead take a night off from CBGB in 1974 to perform a song for the free-flowing composer-musician Frank Zappa on the eve of his birthday.

21 DECEMBER

Saluting Frank Zappa, birthed on the Winter Solstice, a born
Capricorn. Like the high-spirited mountain goat, no one could
pin him down.

22 DECEMBER

Ralph Fiennes, on the set of *Coriolanus*, his directorial debut. A moment before entering a confrontational scene, the inner director counsels the brooding actor.

23 DECEMBER

The ruins of Hadrian's great library, which once housed over
17,000 works. How wonderful the worlds we enter through the
words of others; how tragic our loss of them.

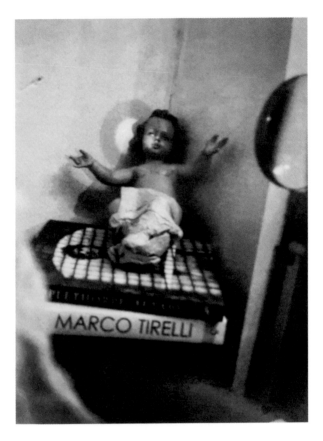

24 DECEMBER

On Christmas Eve we contemplate the birth of a child, the hope of the world.

PATTi's First BirthDAY

25 DECEMBER

My first Christmas, Chicago, 1947. On that afternoon, I walked across the kitchen for the first time, spurred on by my mother waving a new toy rabbit.

26 DECEMBER

Memories of work past, divining work future.

27 DECEMBER

Young goat in Senegal. Capricorn blessings to Lenny Kaye and
Oliver Ray, both born on this day.

28 DECEMBER

We seek the smallest of oracles: what fate offers, how everything connects. Turning each card, I find assurance as well as intense challenges and the stamina and discipline to face them.

29 DECEMBER

Now to place energy into the task at hand.
Happy birthday to Ann Demeulemeester.
Ceaselessly creating.

30 DECEMBER

Every birthday, my
mother would call me
at 6:01 in the morning
and leave this message:
Wake up, Patricia,
you are born.

31 DECEMBER

Happy New Year,
everybody! We are
alive together.

All Polaroids, cell images, and drawings are by Patti Smith, from the P.S. Archives, or in the public domain, save those acknowledged below. I extend my admiration and gratitude to the following:

KLAUS BIESENBACH | PS at Rockaway Beach **1**

UNICEF/UNI325447/HELLBERG | Greta Thunberg **3**

RALPH CRANE. LIFE ARCHIVES | Flag insert of Joan Baez **9**

YOICHI R. OKAMOTO (WHPO) | Martin Luther King **15**

STEVEN SEBRING | PS room **29** • *Finnegans Wake* **44** • Empire State Building **86** • PS with phone **88** • Earth Day **116** • PS with Polaroid **156** • PS, Jesse Jackson **294**

COURTESY OF BEVERLY PEPPER PROJECTS FOUNDATION **39**

JESSE PARIS SMITH | Snowman **49** • Self-Picture **93** • PS, Milan **359**

BOB GRUEN | Yoko Ono in Central Park, 1973 **50**

ANTON CORBIN | Kurt Cobain **52**

ALLEN GINSBERG ESTATE | PS with William Burroughs **37**

JACK PETRUZZELLI | PS with Lenny Kaye, Byron Bay **60**

TONY SPINA | PS with Fred Sonic Smith, Detroit **63**

SIMONE MERLI | PS with Werner Herzog **67**

MOTT CARTER/CLAY MATHEMATICS INSTITUTE | Maryam Mirzakhani **70**

DAVID BELISLE | PS with Michael Stipe, New York City **74**

ALLAN ARBUS | Photograph of Diane Arbus, c. 1949 © The Estate of Diane Arbus **76**

KAREN SHEINHEIT | Tony Shanahan **79** • Jay Dee Daugherty **84**

ARCHIVIO MARIO SCHIFANO | Frank O'Hara **87**

Anna Akhmatova, *Requiem, Poem Without a Hero*

Ryunosuke Akutagawa, *Rashomon and Seventeen Other Stories*

Diane Arbus, *Revelations*

Antonin Artaud, *Artaud Anthology*

Thomas Bernhard, *The Loser, Wittgenstein's Nephew*

Roberto Bolaño, *2666, Amulet*

Herman Broch, *The Death of Virgil*

Emily Brontë, *Wuthering Heights*

Mikhail Bulgakov, *The Master and Margarita*

William S. Burroughs, *The Wild Boys, Queer*

Albert Camus, *A Happy Death, The First Man*

Carlo Collodi, *Pinocchio*

Gregory Corso, *The Happy Birthday of Death*

Stéphan Crasneanscki, *What We Leave Behind*

Osamu Dazai, *No Longer Human*

Emily Dickenson, *The Complete Poems*

Joan Didion, *Play It as It Lays*

Marguerite Duras, *The Lover, Writing*

Isabelle Eberhardt, *The Oblivion Seekers*

David Edmonds and John Eidinow, *Bobby Fischer Goes to War*

T. S. Eliot, *Collected Poems*

Jean Genet, *The Thief's Journal*

Allen Ginsberg, *Collected Poems 1947–1980*

Nikolai Gogol, *The Overcoat and Other Tales*

Janet Hamill, *A Map of the Heavens*

385

Marlen Haushofer, *The Wall*

Hayden Herrera, *Frida: A Biography of Frida Kahlo*

Hermann Hesse, *The Journey to the East*

Anna Kavan, *Ice, Julia and the Bazooka*

Lenny Kaye, *Lightning Striking*

Martin Luther King, Jr., *A Testament of Hope*

H. P. Lovecraft, *At the Mountains of Madness*

Henning Mankell, Wallander series

Yukio Mishima, *Confessions of a Mask, Star*

Haruki Murakami, *The Wind-Up Bird Chronicle*

Vladimir Nabokov, *Nikolai Gogol*

Gérard de Nerval, *Aurélia, The Women of Cairo*

Sylvia Plath, *Ariel, The Colossus*

Maria Popova, *Figuring*

Marcel Proust, *Swann in Love*

John Richardson, *A Life of Picasso*

Gerhard Richter, *The Daily Practice of Painting*

Arthur Rimbaud, *A Season in Hell, Illuminations*

Rumi, *Mystical Poems of Rumi*

Albertine Sarrazin, *Astragal, Runaway*

Bruno Schulz, *The Street of Crocodiles*

Mary Shelley, *Frankenstein; or, The Modern Prometheus*

Susan Sontag, *The Volcano Lover*

Dylan Thomas, *Portrait of the Artist as a Young Dog*

Anne Waldman, *Gossamurmur*

e.g. walker, *Stinky Puppets, Chronicles of Lucy*

Robert Walser, *Berlin Stories, Looking at Pictures*

Edmund White, *Genet: A Biography*

Walt Whitman, *Leaves of Grass*

Virginia Woolf, *The Waves, The Collected Essays of Virginia Woolf*

ABOUT THE AUTHOR

PATTI SMITH is the author of the National Book Award winner *Just Kids,* as well as *Woolgathering, M Train, Year of the Monkey,* and numerous collections of poetry and essays. Her seminal album *Horses* has been hailed as one of the top 100 albums of all time. Her global exhibitions include Strange Messenger, Land 250, Camera Solo, Veils, and 18 Stations. The French Ministry of Culture awarded Smith the title of Commandeur des Arts et des Lettres in 2005. Inducted into the Rock & Roll Hall of Fame in 2007, Smith is also the recipient of the ASCAP Founders Award, Sweden's Polar Prize for significant achievements in music, and the PEN America Literary Service Award.